Weddings
101

HONOR
B O O K S

Honor Books
Tulsa, Oklahoma

Weddings 101
ISBN 1-56292-580-6
Copyright © 2001 by Honor Books
P.O. Box 55388
Tulsa, Oklahoma 74155

Manuscript written and compiled by Debra Wong and Sue Rhodes Dodd.

Introduction

*W*hether you are the bride or the groom, your wedding will be one of the most significant events in your life. Every detail should be perfect, every dream fulfilled, every moment a cherished memory.

This inspiring little book has been designed to help make your wedding all that you want it to be. The tips on wedding planning and etiquette are sure to save you time and energy. We have also included creative, fun, and inspiring ideas to help make this special day uniquely yours.

May God bless you as you celebrate your mutual commitment and begin your journey down life's road together.

Engaging Issues

*So, you're engaged! Here are some helpful tips
to get you started on planning your wedding.*

*B*eyond Your Wildest Dreams

He finally popped the question. His words are recorded forever in your heart. You can't take your eyes off your left hand. Congratulations! A lifetime of happiness! Everyone offers his or her well wishes. Receive the compliments, bask in the moment, and allow yourself to savor the joys of engagement.

Once you come down from cloud nine, it's time to start thinking about the wedding day. Use the first few weeks of your engagement to dream big.

Start by envisioning the wedding of a lifetime. Imagine all the glorious details without regard to cost. Reality and budget can be dealt with once your actual planning time gets underway. This is the time to hope beyond your wildest dreams.

I will make you my wife forever,
showing you righteousness and justice,
unfailing love and compassion.
I will be faithful to you and make you mine.

—*Hosea 2:19-20* NLT

Engaging Issues

You're engaged and want to tell the whole world your exciting news. So why not do it?

- ♥ Declare the good news to family first.
- ♥ Share your engagement with friends.
- ♥ Inform co-workers and boss.
- ♥ Write a short article to communicate your engagement with the public.
- ♥ Have an engagement photo taken to accompany the announcement.
- ♥ Submit your news to the local newspaper, alumni magazine, church communicator, and organizational newsletters.

Love is, above all, the gift of oneself.

—Jean Anouilh

Engaging Issues

Your engagement time is the first step in the rest of your life together. Involve God from day one. Here are a few ideas to get you started.

1. Pray at the meals you share together.
2. Read a book together and discuss it.
3. Ask one another how you can pray for him or her.
4. Join a Bible study together.
5. Find a married couple from your church to mentor you.

It's normal for the engagement to be
peppered with fear, tension, and discord.
It's normal to feel inadequate compared to the fairy tale.
But the only real source of splendor is faith,
holding on to your groom's hand,
and choosing the great unknown.

—*Marg Stark*

Engaging Issues

Anastacia was enjoying the coastal drive to visit Tim's parents. Today their normal route took a new turn. Tim stopped the car at a park overlooking the Pacific Ocean. When he pulled his guitar from the trunk, she knew what would happen next.

As they sat down on a shaded bench, Tim unfolded a piece of paper containing the words to "You Are," a song he wrote for Anastacia. Her eyes filled with tears as his trembling voice warmed her heart.

You are the stars in my sky,
you are the sparkle in my eye.

The song concluded with Tim kneeling, presenting her with a diamond ring, and asking hopefully: "Will you be my wife?"

Dreaming together is like marriage insurance:
You're blending your hopes for a shared future.

—Annette LaPlaca

Marriage is a journey, not a destination.
It's a marathon, not a sprint.
It's a lifetime union of two imperfect
people who love each other.

—Claudia Arp

*Discuss your feelings with
your fiancé, friends, and family.*

You are in a transitional time of life.

Lean on those you love.

I love you, not only for what you are,
But for what I am when I am with you.

—*Roy Croft*

Weddings ·•101·•·

*May he give you the desire of your heart
and make all your plans succeed.*
—Psalm 20:4

*In his heart a man plans his course,
but the LORD determines his steps.*
—Proverbs 16:9

Engaging Issues

Plan a "dream" date—a special time set aside for you and your fiancé to dream about your wedding day.

Write your ideas down on paper.

Revisit the list as you begin planning the big event.

It was so very good of God to let my dreams come true,
to note a young girl's cherished hopes
then lead her right to you.

—Ruth Bell Graham

Engaging Issues

You can't make any of your plans—booking a florist, hiring a photographer, ordering invitations—until you do the following:

- ♥ Set your wedding date
- ♥ Reserve the church
- ♥ Place a hold on the reception hall
- ♥ Confirm your pastor's availability

When she saw the dress, her eyes echoed her squeal of delight. Her mother told her she could try it on "just this once."

She slipped the adult size six dress over her child size seven frame. "Mother, it's so beautiful. I feel like a fairy princess."

Her mind completed the outfit—a veil covering her face, a large bouquet of pink roses, ballet slippers on her feet, and to top it off, a sparkling diamond solitaire on her hand.

Although her wedding was still years away, she began planning it the day she tried on her mother's wedding dress.

Engaging Issues

You are still in the early planning stages of your wedding. Take the time to do the following:

- ♥ Celebrate
- ♥ Dream together
- ♥ Pray about your upcoming decisions
- ♥ Relax
- ♥ Have fun

I pray that your love for each
other will overflow more and more,
and that you will keep on growing
in your knowledge and understanding.

—*Philippians 1:9* NLT

Engaging Issues

Don't let your marriage be the end of your discovery of one another. Take the time to probe deeper into the heart of your mate. Spend your life seeking to know your spouse's thoughts, feelings, and deepest desires. Begin by sharing your own hopes with your fiancé.

The man who finds a wife finds a good thing;
she is a blessing to him from the Lord.

—*Proverbs 18:22* TLB

I wish you the blessing of God for a good beginning
and a steadfast middle time,
and may you hold out until a blessed end,
this all in and through Jesus Christ.
Amen.

—Amish Blessing

Planning Early On

*Weddings take a lot of time, cash, and energy.
Plan early, so you can enjoy your celebration more!*

Planning Early On

Budget the Best

"Best" does not always mean expensive, nor does it always mean elaborate. It is highly subjective and should reflect your personal preferences. There are dozens of books on the market providing extensive advice on wedding planning and watching expenses.

It is possible to have the wedding of your dreams without going bankrupt. With careful research and planning, you can probably "have it all"—or at least *most* of it. Decide which aspects of the wedding are the most important for you and set your budget accordingly. Do this in advance—before you start meeting with vendors, some of whom have a vested interest in parting you from your pocketbook.

Think about it. Do you want a high-end designer dress at the high-end designer price? Or can you find virtually the same thing through a reputable bargain broker? Do you want an elaborate reception (with a cost of $50 per guest or more), or would hors d'oeuvres and cake do the trick?

Do your homework, and you'll likely save a bundle.

Now glory be to God who by his mighty power at work within us is able to do far more than we would ever dare to ask or even dream of—infinitely beyond our highest prayers, desires, thoughts, or hopes.
—Ephesians 3:20 TLB

In marriage, as in all things, contentment excels wealth.
—Moliére

*Planning a wedding together can
help you explore your values,
set priorities, learn the art of compromise,
work in tandem for a common purpose,
and deal with real life money issues.*
—Eileen Silva Kindig

*If your plans as a couple are
to have value and potential,
then God must be involved in
that planning through prayer.*

—Judy Douglass

Planning Early On

"I will pray for your communication to be open."

"We pray that you are filled with joy."

"I'll pray for ease in adjusting."

Ronda and Gary's hearts were full of joy and their eyes brimmed with tears as they read through the prayer cards. At the wedding reception, guests filled out cards stating how they would pray for the newlyweds over the next year.

Ronda and Gary's entire relationship was rooted in prayer. They wanted to carry that foundation into their wedding and marriage. Every aspect of their wedding was bathed in prayer. On her wedding day, Ronda exclaimed, "Every detail came out more perfectly than I could have ever dreamed."

Rich or poor, or somewhere in between,
the bride planning a formal wedding
is ready to spend not only money
but time and thought
in choosing the dress of her dreams.
—Alice Lea Mast Tasman

Planning Early On

Even if your heart is set on a fitted dress with spaghetti straps, take the time to try on many styles of wedding dresses. You will be surprised what styles you actually like. Visit various bridal stores. Invite a friend to join you for each excursion. After a few shopping trips, one dress will stand out in your mind.

Come to me,
all you who are
weary and burdened,
and I will give you rest.
—*Matthew 11:28*

Plan days of rest.
Set a rule that you won't do any wedding planning on those days.
You need times of rejuvenation to keep your energy up and your focus clear.

I've always said, if you don't have a fortune,
rather than doing ten things on the skinny,
pick three things and
do them well.

—*Colin Cowie*

But their trust should be in the living God,
who richly gives us all we need for our enjoyment.

—1 Timothy 6:17 NLT

Planning Early On

Set your budget for each of the items on this list. Prices will vary based on your geographic location. If you are unsure what a realistic amount is, call a few vendors in your area to get a quote for the current rates.

- ♥ Ceremony/reception rental
- ♥ Invitations
- ♥ Flowers
- ♥ Photography/videography
- ♥ Bride's and groom's attire
- ♥ Hors d'oeuvres/meal/cake

- ♥ Music
- ♥ Wedding programs/party favors
- ♥ Wedding rings
- ♥ Gifts for wedding party
- ♥ Limousine
- ♥ Rehearsal dinner

When choosing your photographer, keep in mind that you will be spending your entire wedding day with this person. As a couple, discuss the following questions:

1. Did we feel comfortable when we met with the photographer?
2. Was the photographer accommodating when we made unique requests?
3. Did the photographer offer helpful suggestions to enhance our wedding day and not force ideas upon us?
4. Were we able to get a list of previous customers to contact for references?
5. Were the prices reasonable, or were there extra charges for every special request?

Planning Early On

*Whenever you begin to feel tense,
look at the big picture—celebrating
your commitment to your fiancé
in front of those who love you—
and don't sweat the small stuff,
which is not bad advice for marriage in general.*

—Bernadette Starzee

One of the most difficult tasks in wedding planning is paring down your guest list to fit the style and budget of your wedding. One rule of thumb is to let the groom's family invite one-third of the guests, the bride's family one-third of the guests, and the bride and groom together choose the other one-third.

It's the small accessories (guest book, garter, slip, purse, gloves, cake server, etc.) that often throw the budget off. If possible, make your own or borrow these items. This can save you not only a few hundred dollars but also the time it takes to shop for them.

Often, the things in life that
seem to be the most effortless
are the ones that require the most preparation.
—Lisa Carse

June means weddings in everyone's lexicon,
Weddings in Swedish, weddings in Mexican.
Breezes play Mendelssohn, treeses play Youmans,
Birds wed birds, and humans wed humans.
All year long the gentlemen woo,
But the ladies dream of a June "I do."
Ladies grow loony, and gentlemen loonier;
This year's June is next year's Junior.
                                    —Ogden Nash

Planning Early On

Celia gazed out the window of the airplane and let her mind wander back. She and Brett had been married for about three months now, and what a wonderful three months it had been.

In order to stay out of credit card debt but still have the wedding of their dreams, Brett and Celia planned their wedding in stages. Celia's face softened as her thoughts drifted back to their intimate wedding at a Bed and Breakfast with their parents, Brett's oldest brother, who was also the minister, and his wife. She chuckled when she remembered the reception for family and friends six weeks after the wedding. What a fun night! Now here they were, several weeks later, headed for their honeymoon.

She leaned over and placed a gentle kiss on her husband's cheek and whispered, "Happy wedding day, my love."

If you are following tradition, the groom and his family are responsible to pay for the items listed on the following page. The bride and her family cover the other expenses. However, if someone wants to contribute toward your wedding, accept the generous offer over tradition.

Planning Early On

- ❤ Bride's engagement and wedding rings
- ❤ Gift for the bride
- ❤ Gifts for the best man and ushers
- ❤ Groom's wedding attire
- ❤ Marriage license
- ❤ Clergyman's fee
- ❤ Boutonnieres for the men in the wedding party
- ❤ Bride's bouquet
- ❤ Corsages for mothers and grandmothers
- ❤ Rehearsal dinner
- ❤ Honeymoon

Celebrating Your Wedding

*Your wedding is one of the most precious days
of your life. Make yours memorable and
a true reflection of both bride and groom.*

Express Yourself

Does the bride's taste lean toward formal and traditional? Informal and avant-garde? Simple and elegant? Lush and elaborate? Here is your chance to express your own personal style throughout the wedding.

A formal/traditional bride may prefer to enter a cathedral in a formal dress to the majestic chords of Mendelssohn's "Bridal Chorus." Another bride may prefer flowers in her hair, bare feet, and a stroll on the beach. Another may prefer jeans, boots, and a fleet of motorcycles.

Then, there are the "little" issues. Do you want to carry a cascading bouquet, a single bud, or a group of "just-picked" flowers? Do you want a sit-down formal dinner, or would a simple "cake-and-punch" reception suffice? Do you want albums of candid photos, formal ones, or some combination of both? Will the reception play alternative music, country and western, classical, or '50s rock 'n' roll?

Remember, each decision should reflect the style and personality of the bride and groom, as their budgets will allow.

*A prerequisite for doing a wedding your way
is opening up your mind
so that you're not restricted by
traditional wedding options.*

—Danielle Claro

Celebrating Your Wedding

Consider hiring a wedding consultant to help you create a wedding that is uniquely you.

Frank J. Andonoplas, an accredited bridal consultant in Chicago, describes his role:

"I can help create the atmosphere that the bride is looking for and maybe come up with some fresh ideas that she never even knew were available. I'm really kind of a bride's right arm. I have done hundreds of weddings, and I know what works and how it should work. I have even helped brides and grooms out of some real jams at times."

When you love someone,
all your saved-up wishes start coming out.
—Elizabeth Bowen

A wedding should automatically be personalized.
It's not just another party;
it's the appropriate opportunity to tell people
who you are and what you are about.
—Colin Cowie

Celebrating Your Wedding

To help you figure out what style of wedding you want, choose three words from the list below that describe you and your fiancé:

Fun	Contemporary
Romantic	Musical
Casual	Witty
Formal	Warm
Elegant	Relaxed
Spontaneous	Small
Spiritual	Stylish
Trendy	Artistic
Chic	Dramatic
Family-oriented	Upbeat
Traditional	Old-fashioned
Lavish	Energized

—Caroll Stoner

*If you remain in me
and my words remain in you,
ask whatever you wish,
and it will be given you.*

—*John 15:7*

Celebrating Your Wedding

Select a few of your most cherished wedding dreams.
Discuss your ideas with friends and family.
Come up with a list of steps to make your desires reality.
Invest your time and energy to make them happen.

Think of your wedding day as a worship service.
Include rituals used in your Sunday morning service—

> worship songs,
> communion,
> scripture reading,
> prayer,
> symbolic candles.

That there is something intrinsically
sacred in the marriage contract
is evidenced by the fact that all religions,
even the most corrupt,
always have regarded it as such
and surrounded it with religious rites and ceremonies.

—K.J.I. Hochban

Celebrating Your Wedding

Balancing Act

One of the unique challenges of a wedding is balancing romance and reverence with personal preferences and tradition. Aside from certain legal requirements to meet government ordinances and certain restrictions associated with a particular house of worship, the wedding ceremony itself has limitless options.

If you choose to wed in a house of worship, you will have to comply with the "rules of the house," so to speak, with regard to music selection, on-site festivities, prayers, vows, and any other traditions. If you choose another location, consider incorporating any reverent observances that will make your wedding the holy and precious event it is.

Once you have established your personal style and preferences and determined the requirements/restrictions associated with your event, research the various elements of weddings and create your own unique combination.

God is love.

—1 John 4:8

Husbands,
love your wives,
just as Christ loved the church
and gave himself up for her.

—Ephesians 5:25

We need our traditions and rituals to remind
us as individuals and as a community
that being married is more than filing
joint income tax and sharing a mortgage.
We need them to remind us that we are spiritual beings
deeply loved by God
and deeply connected to one another.
—Eileen Silva Kindig

Love each other with genuine affection,
and take delight in honoring each other.

—*Romans 12:10* NLT

Celebrating Your Wedding

Their wedding was one of the most unique ever seen. They didn't throw out tradition altogether but merged the new with the old. The bride and groom wore traditional attire, yet each bridesmaid chose her own black dress in a style that flattered her figure. The choir loft was full—not with singers but with a handful of the bride and groom's closest friends. Their duty was to literally stand with the happy couple throughout the wedding ceremony and figuratively throughout their marriage.

The reception kept with the theme of old and new combined. Each table was assigned to a friend who took the role of hostess, designer, and baker. The individually decorated tables included a homemade wedding cake as the centerpiece. Dinner consisted of your choice of one of four food stations: Greek, Italian, Chinese, and good old-fashioned American barbecue. The combination of tradition and contemporary hit its peak when the bride and her father began moonwalking to Michael Jackson's "Beat It."

Daisy, Daisy, give me your answer, do!
I'm half crazy, all for the love of you!
It won't be a stylish marriage,
I can't afford a carriage,
But you'll look sweet upon the seat
Of a bicycle built for two!
—Harry Dacre

Celebrating Your Wedding

Your transportation to/from the reception is a great place to show your individuality. Choose your mode of transportation from the following list of ideas:

Limousine

Rolls Royce

Vintage car

Horse-drawn carriage

Hot air balloon

Trolley car

Helicopter

Gondola

Taxicab

Bus

Personal vehicle

Friend's car

Motorcycle

Roller skates

Skis

Hay wagon

Boat

Bicycle built for two

Your wedding day is a day to honor one another, your family and friends, and God. Below are a few traditional and some unique ways to accomplish this.

- ♥ Surprise your fiancé by singing a song.
- ♥ Give your mothers a flower and a kiss.
- ♥ Buy individualized gifts for each member of the wedding party.
- ♥ Include a time of worship.
- ♥ Write your own vows.
- ♥ Have your father walk you down the aisle.

Celebrating Your Wedding

- ♥ Wear your mother's wedding dress.
- ♥ Let your bridesmaids choose their own dresses.
- ♥ Ask each father to offer a blessing for the newly formed family.
- ♥ Have a bridesmaid and a groomsman luncheon.
- ♥ Buy your future spouse a wedding gift.
- ♥ Use your grandmother's ring for your wedding band.

Love is
the excitement of planning things together
the excitement of doing things together.
Love is
the source of the future.
—Susan Polis Schutz

Celebrating Your Wedding

For each planned wedding detail, ask yourself this series of questions to confirm that you are creating a wedding that truly reflects the both of you:

1. Is this a reflection of my fiancé and/or me?
2. Was this chosen to honor a member of our family?
3. Did we include this detail purely for tradition's sake?
4. Would either of us regret removing this item from our wedding day?

Overcoming the Obstacles

Let's face it—not everything is going to progress smoothly. Sometimes tempers flare and emotions get heated. Here are some ideas to help you keep your cool.

Overcoming the Obstacles

First Steps

When you think of a wedding, what words come to your mind? Stress? Tension? Frustration? Anger? Of course not! Unfortunately, these words ring true for some during their engagement. However, there are ways to ensure they don't describe your personal experience.

Wedding planning is one of the best opportunities for you and your fiancé to learn the delicate balance of compromise, the rewards of honest communication, and the gift of forgiveness. The obstacles you overcome at this time will equip you to handle future difficulties in your life. The first step toward the wedding of your dreams is learning how to be kind, understanding, and open. It's also great preparation for the marriage of a lifetime.

*You don't want to remember the months
spent planning your wedding with a grimace.
This is an ideal time to strengthen bonds
with family and friends,
while kicking off good relationships with your new in-
laws. By taking steps now to avoid
stress and hurt feelings,
you can pave the way to a blissful wedding
and strong family ties for years to come.*

—Lambeth Hochwald

Overcoming the Obstacles

Bless us, Lord, as we weather this family conflict.
We all have certain needs to be met,
certain ways of trying to fulfill our dreams.
Yet each of us seeks this one basic thing in the midst of it all:

Love.

Simply love.

—Gary Wilde

Kindness in words creates confidence.
Kindness in thinking creates profoundness.
Kindness in giving creates love.

—*Chinese proverb*

Overcoming the Obstacles

To reduce the chance of hurting the feelings of important family members and friends, honor them with a special place in your wedding. You can invite them to do any of the following:

- ❤ Attend to gifts
- ❤ Distribute wedding programs
- ❤ Light candles
- ❤ Greet guests at the ceremony and/or reception site
- ❤ Supply goodies to the bride's room before the ceremony
- ❤ Read scripture
- ❤ Perform a song during the ceremony or reception

Be completely humble and gentle;
be patient,
bearing with one another in love.
Make every effort to keep the unity of the Spirit
through the bond of peace.
—*Ephesians 4:2-3*

Overcoming the Obstacles

Nuptial Negotiations

As early as possible in the planning process, the bride and groom should set out their own priorities. Plenty of people—some well meaning and some merely trying to close a sale—will offer solicited and unsolicited advice as you plan your wedding. Have a clear idea of what parts of the wedding are in your "top priority" category, which ones are optional (or negotiable), and which ones you do not plan to include.

Once you have that foundation firmly in place, discuss your hopes and dreams with the people who will be footing the bill. And remember these two facts:

1. The wedding is for the bride and groom. Their wishes should be incorporated into the wedding wherever good taste, family consideration, and the pocketbook allow.
2. Whoever is footing the bill always gets a vote on the outcome.

*The genius of communication is the ability to be
both totally honest and totally kind at the same time.*

—*John Powell*

Overcoming the Obstacles

Love is patient and kind.
Love is not jealous or boastful or proud or rude.
Love does not demand its own way.
Love is not irritable,
and it keeps no record of when it has been wronged.
It is never glad about injustice
but rejoices whenever the truth wins out.
Love never gives up,
never loses faith,
is always hopeful,
and endures through every circumstance.
—1 Corinthians 13:4-7 NLT

If I see conflict as natural, neutral, normal,
I may be able to see the difficulties we experience
as tension in relationships and
honest differences in perspective
that can be worked through
by caring about each other and
confronting each other
with truth expressed by love.

—*David Augsburger*

Overcoming the Obstacles

*If we had no winter,
the spring would not be so pleasant:
if we did not sometimes taste of adversity,
prosperity would not be so welcome.*
—*Anne Bradstreet*

*Before the situation spins out of control,
stop and take a deep breath—
don't forget why you're getting married!*
—*Leah Ingram*

Dear Lord,

We are facing so much today. We aren't sure which decision is the right one. We ask for Your guidance and wisdom. Show us how You want this wedding to be. We want to honor one another, our family, and You through this whole process. Teach us how to communicate more clearly with one another. Make Your presence known to us. Help us to remember to turn to You before things get out of control. Thank you for Your love for us and our love for each other. We ask for Your continued presence in our lives before, during, and after our wedding.

Amen.

Overcoming the Obstacles

Be quick to listen, slow to speak and slow to become angry.

—James 1:19

With so many details to coordinate, stress is likely to knock you off your feet at times. Here are a few suggestions to overcome stress and catch conflict before it starts:

- ♥ Stop
- ♥ Slow down
- ♥ Delegate tasks
- ♥ Talk to someone
- ♥ Schedule time for exercise
- ♥ Distract yourself with things you enjoy
- ♥ Take a short walk to clear your head
- ♥ Identify the source of your stress
- ♥ Have a power nap
- ♥ Read the Bible
- ♥ Breathe deeply
- ♥ Pray

When care comes,
we will laugh it away,
or if the load is too heavy
we will sit down and share it between us
till it becomes almost as light as pleasure itself.
—*Sir Walter Scott*

A happy marriage is the union of two good forgivers.
—Ruth Bell Graham

Love is an act of endless forgiveness,
a tender look which becomes a habit.
—Peter Ustinov

Two are better than one,
because they have a good return for their work:
If one falls down,
his friend can help him up.
—*Ecclesiastes 4:9-10*

Overcoming the Obstacles

"How am I going to sell my house, pack, and plan a wedding in three months?" Debbie was feeling like most brides-to-be during their engagement—overwhelmed.

Robert responded with rational advice that went right past Debbie. "There's just so much to do," she sobbed.

Robert realized practical suggestions weren't working, so he changed his tactic. "Well, we could have our reception in the moving truck. Everyone can pack up your house, jump in the van, and we'll serve wedding cake at our new home."

Debbie's eyes began to sparkle, and her mouth turned upward into a smile. She knew whatever problems they'd face in the future, they would face them together with smiles on their faces.

Never blame.
Take responsibility for your part in the problem.
Accept the apology and grant forgiveness.
Kiss and make up.

Overcoming the Obstacles

Make us of one heart and mind,
Courteous, merciful, and kind;
Lowly, meek in thought and word,
Ne'er by fretful passion stirred.
Free from anger, free from pride,
Let us thus in God abide;
All the depth of love express,
All the height of holiness.

—*Charles Wesley*

Love does not consist in gazing at each other,
but in looking outward in the same direction.
—Antoine de Saint-Exupery

Become a united front.
Stand up for one another's dreams and goals.
You will become one when you are married.
Start developing that oneness now.

The courage to share your feelings is critical to
sustaining a love relationship.
—Harold H. Bloomfield

The best way to avoid conflict is clear communication. Run through the following questions in your mind before, during, and after opening your mouth:

- ♥ **Identify your feelings:** Am I disappointed, frustrated, tired, embarrassed, or pressured?
- ♥ **Communicate your feelings:** Did I speak clearly, accusingly, or defensively?
- ♥ **Listen to the receiver's response:** Was I understood?
- ♥ **End the conversation on a positive note:** How can I affirm the receiver?

Overcoming the Obstacles

We're getting the wedding we want,
plus something more important:
a closer bond.
All that talk, all those decisions, all the compromises
required a lot of patience and understanding.
At its deepest level,
the planning process,
I now realize,
is actually about committing to each other.
—Eric Messinger

Getting Ready for the Ceremony

The clock is ticking, and your big day is almost here!
Have you thought of everything?

*D*elegate, Delegate, Delegate

The few weeks before your wedding are packed solid. You'll need to get the final guest count to the caterer, make a seating chart, pay the vendors, pick up your dress, and so on. The final days before your wedding are usually spent greeting out-of-town guests, wrapping gifts for the wedding party, attending the rehearsal, and trying to stay calm. You have been planning for months, and the last details are now being finalized.

From the rehearsal onward, the bride and groom should be free from responsibility. Use the last week or so before your wedding day to tie up loose ends, and hand off all responsibilities to others. Allow those who love you to carry the load. Schedule time to relax with your family and friends who are sharing this time with you. Run through each detail to ensure that you will be free to absorb, and appreciate every moment when your actual wedding day arrives.

Something old,
something new,
Something borrowed,
something blue.
—*Victorian rhyme*

Getting Ready for the Ceremony

Figure out what your old, new, borrowed, and blue will be in advance. Here are a few ideas:

- A handkerchief made from the lace on your mother's wedding dress
- A piece of jewelry that's a family heirloom
- A new penny with the year of your wedding on it
- The bracelet your fiancé gave you as a wedding gift
- Your wedding dress
- Your great-grandmother's pearls that belong to your mother
- A friend's petticoat
- A garter laced with blue ribbon
- A blue pendant necklace
- A single blue flower tucked into your all-white bouquet

God is the silent partner in all great enterprises.

—Abraham Lincoln

And be sure of this:
I am with you always,
even to the end of the age.

—Matthew 28:20 NLT

Getting Ready for the Ceremony

The wedding invitations were finally in the mail. However, the young bride had a nagging feeling she had forgotten someone. She checked and rechecked the list. Everyone was accounted for. She called her fiancé to see if he could think of anyone.

"Well, there is one other person we forgot to send an invitation to." He seemed hesitant to continue.

"Who is it?" she insisted, eyes scanning the list again. He cleared his throat and with a soft voice whispered, "God." Her task-mode mentality quickly shifted to one of peace.

When she filled out the envelope on this last invitation, the address simply read:

God
c/o Heaven

Love has nothing to do with what you are expecting to get, it's what you are expected to give—which is everything.

—Anonymous

It is more blessed to give than to receive.

—Acts 20:35

Getting Ready for the Ceremony

Do everything possible beforehand so you can avoid the pressure of handling details on your wedding day. Delegate as many responsibilities as possible to others. Do a wedding-day schedule. Ask a friend to watch details, trust your mother, or hire a consultant.

—Carroll Stoner

Keep a notebook detailing the plans and important elements of the wedding.

Glance over it again to confirm you have covered everything.

Assign someone to each vendor.

Provide that person with a copy of the information you have in your notebook.

I…chose my wife, as she did her
wedding-gown, not for a fine glossy surface,
but such qualities as would wear well.
—Oliver Goldsmith

*But almost without exception,
couples feel a certain sense of confidence and calm
when they finally reach the altar
and prepare to take part in the ceremony
that will bring them together forever.*

—Lisa Carse

*During Elizabethan times, it was common
for the two main bridesmaids to come to the
bride's room the morning of the ceremony to
dress her, while the groomsmen would be at the
groom's house trimming his hair and beard and
adorning him with flowers and ribbons.*

—*Sydney Barbara Metrick*

Getting Ready for the Ceremony

Sandy breathed deeply to inhale the aroma of Darjeeling tea and peach scones. She gladly took the role of matron of honor but never anticipated a bridesmaid tea. Wasn't this her time to spoil her sister and not be spoiled herself?

Each of the bridesmaids had known Sandy's sister a long time, but *she* held the candle for knowing her longest. Sandy was six when her sister was born. It was always her job to pass on her knowledge and to assist her little sister in life.

Sandy remembered the many years she thought her baby sister was such a pain and nuisance. Now she looked at her sister, maybe for the first time, as an adult. It was just a few weeks before the wedding, yet the focus was on honoring friends—not the bride. Sandy paused and prayed a silent thanks. After all these years, they were not just sisters, but had become *friends* too.

I am overwhelmed with joy in the L<small>ORD</small> my God!
For he has dressed me with the clothing of salvation
and draped me in a robe of righteousness.
I am like a bridegroom in his wedding suit
or a bride with her jewels.

—Isaiah 61:10 <small>NLT</small>

Getting Ready for the Ceremony

Arrange for help on your wedding day—give each bridesmaid a different task. Here are a few items they can assist you with:

- 💝 Help you get dressed.
- 💝 Apply touchups to your makeup when necessary.
- 💝 Carry bobby pins to hold up falling hair.
- 💝 Lead a prayer before the ceremony starts.
- 💝 Bring munchies for the bride's room.

The marriage ceremony isn't like graduation;
rather, it's similar to the first day of kindergarten!
Its not the culmination,
but the beginning.

—Susan Alexander Yates

Getting Ready for the Ceremony

Celebrate this transition in life. Have a tasteful bachelorette party.

- ♥ See a play.
- ♥ Go out to a trendy restaurant.
- ♥ Plan an old-fashioned slumber party.

Enjoy a night of harmless fun with your girlfriends.

We can complain because rose bushes have thorns
or rejoice because thorn bushes have roses.

—Dag Hammarskjöld

Getting Ready for the Ceremony

Prayer, preparation, and a positive attitude are the keys to any successful endeavor. Pray for the details of your wedding to go smoothly. Prepare a bridal emergency kit to take care of the minor things. For the big things, just smile and let it go.

Needle and thread
Extra pantyhose
Nail polish and accessories
Hair spray and accessories
Toothbrush and toothpaste
Breath mints
Iron/steamer
Safety pins

Masking tape
Extra earrings
Name and phone number of all
   vendors
Bottled water
Small first-aid kit
Energy bars

Keep the morning of your wedding free of details. Use this time to pray, journal, collect your thoughts, have a good breakfast, and pamper yourself. If you do, you will find yourself floating on clouds all day long.

Getting Ready for the Ceremony

One of the best things to do well in advance is to pack for your honeymoon. Make a list of what you want to bring and check it off as you put it in your suitcase. Add your toiletries and other last minute items the morning of your wedding. Below is a basic list of items to pack that can be adapted for your destination, activities, and the time of year:

camera/video camera/film
prescription medicine
1 pair jeans/khakis
1 lightweight jacket/pullover
1 nice sundress
1 little black dress
1 cardigan—for chilly restaurants
4 play shirts
2 swimsuits (1 bikini and 1 one-piece)
1 pair walking shoes/sandals

1 pair evening shoes/sandals
1 evening purse
extra socks, underwear, and bras
toiletries—especially sunscreen
canvas tote bag for
    beach/pool/souvenirs
compact umbrella/rain poncho
and, of course—your nighties

—www.theknot.com

Don't worry about anything;
instead, pray about everything.
Tell God what you need,
and thank him for all he has done.
If you do this,
you will experience God's peace,
which is far more wonderful
than the human mind can understand.

—Philippians 4:6-7 NLT

The Marriage Journey

Marriage is a journey, which on this day begins
a commitment to each other, a love that never ends.
You have a choice every day to grow together or apart.
You will travel safely with God's word
and with the love He imparts
as you love each other and travel through the years,
the blessing of your journey
will be your union held most dear.

—Jadine Nollan

Weddings
•◦ 101 ◦•

Enjoying Your Big Day

*This is it—the moment you've been waiting for!
Make every minute a special memory to last a lifetime.*

Enjoying Your Big Day

Enjoy Yourself!

Take time to enjoy your wedding ceremony and reception. After all, this is a gathering of your friends and family. They are here to help both bride and groom celebrate this special occasion.

Make it a point to visit with loved ones during the reception. Too many brides and grooms say they regret not pausing long enough in the rush and excitement to really enjoy this special party of all parties. Schedule time during your reception

festivities to allow for "just visiting" moments with your family and friends. That's as much a part of the wedding reception as throwing the bouquet, tossing the garter, or cutting the cake.

Try to relax and enjoy your day as much as possible. Sometimes the bride and groom are so involved in performing all the functions of the wedding ceremony and the reception festivities that they forget to just sit back and have some fun. If you let go of the details and keep things in perspective, you'll have more memories to savor in the years to come.

Weddings
◆ 101 ◆

This is the day the LORD has made;
let us rejoice and be glad in it.
Psalm 118:24

Just remember to enjoy the day.
Don't get so caught up in all the things to do
that you can't simply enjoy the fact
that you are marrying someone you love.

—Paul Deakins

The bride ...
floating all white beside her father
in the morning shadow of trees,
her veil flowing with laughter.
—D. H. Lawrence

Enjoying Your Big Day

Janette awoke, not to the sounds of birds chirping, but to the pitter-patter of raindrops on her window.

"Not today!" she cried. It was the morning of her outdoor wedding. A rush of details flooded her mind.

She slid from her bed onto her knees. "Lord, I trust that You can clear the skies for my wedding on the hill." With complete confidence God would answer her prayers, Janette prepared herself for the wedding of her dreams.

As she stepped from the antique car onto the slightly damp grass, the sun peered through the clouds. The day was more perfect than imagined.

When Alby and Janette said their "I dos," God smiled upon them and kissed their cheeks with rays of sunlight.

Hallelujah!
For our Lord God Almighty reigns.
Let us rejoice and be glad and give him glory!
For the wedding of the Lamb has come,
and his bride has made herself ready.
Fine linen, bright and clean, was given her to wear.
—*Revelation 19:6-8*

Enjoying Your Big Day

You will smile more today than any other day of your life. Allow your smile to come from deep within. Let the joy in your heart bubble out through giggles, laughter, and tears of happiness.

> The organ booms, the procession begins,
> The rejected suitors square their chins,
> and angels swell the harmonious tide
> of blessings upon the bonnie bride.
> but blessings also on him without whom
> there would be no bride.
> I mean the groom.
>
> —Ogden Nash

As a bridegroom rejoices over his bride,
so will your God rejoice over you.

—Isaiah 62:5

Enjoying Your Big Day

My love,

Today is the day I become your wife and you become my husband. I can't believe it's finally here. All the months of planning are over. I want you to know that whatever today holds, the most important thing is that at the end of the day we will be married. I can't wait to walk down the aisle toward you. I'll get to see your smile and feel your touch when you place the ring on my finger. The words "I do" will be filled with joy and hope for our future. You are the love of my life. See you on the aisle.

With all my heart,
Your bride

*You have stolen my heart, my sister, my bride;
you have stolen my heart with one glance of your eyes,
with one jewel of your necklace.
How delightful is your love, my sister, my bride!
How much more pleasing is your love than wine,
and the fragrance of your perfume than any spice!
Your lips drop sweetness as the honeycomb, my bride;
milk and honey are under your tongue.
The fragrance of your garments is like that of Lebanon.
You are a garden fountain, a well of flowing water
streaming down from Lebanon.*
—Song of Songs 4:9-11, 15

Enjoying Your Big Day

Perspiration dripped from his forehead. Who would have thought one could sweat so much in November? The groom shifted his weight from his right foot to his left foot and back again. The last of the bride's friends had found their place at the altar. The organ blasted forth, the sanctuary doors flew open, and there she stood.

An angel, he thought. Her white dress glowed from the sunlight behind her. Once the doors closed, he saw his bride more clearly. A lump moved to the middle of his throat. He swallowed hard several times, never letting his eyes leave her. As she approached, his heartbeat quickened.

He hadn't heard a sound until his father-in-law-to-be grabbed his hand and said, "She's yours now, son." With those words, she laced her arm through his and smiled up at him.

He whispered, "You are truly beautiful."

Weddings
•♦ 101 ♦•

*But the fact is,
for you to have a wonderful wedding—
one that you and your guests
will look back upon with great happiness—
perfection is not necessary.*

—Bernadette Starzee

Enjoying Your Big Day

A receiving line may seem old fashioned, but greeting your guests isn't. Find a way to say hello to everyone. Use one of the ideas listed below, or create one of your own:

♡ Have a receiving line at the reception.
♡ Dismiss the guests row by row at the ceremony instead of using ushers.
♡ Briefly stop by each table at the reception.
♡ Set up an area where the guests can have a picture taken with the happy couple.

A dream is a wish your heart makes.

—Cinderella

For mem'ry has painted this perfect day
With colors that never fade.

—Carrie Jacobs Bond

Marriage is a promise,
a potential,
made in the hearts of two people who love,
which takes a lifetime to fulfill.
—Edmund O'Neill

Weddings
•▶ 101 ◀•

Capture the images of your wedding day as soon as possible. To help jog your memory, answer the following questions:

- ♡ What was my favorite part of the wedding?
- ♡ How was I feeling at each point of the day?
- ♡ What is my husband's best memory of the day?
- ♡ Which elements of the wedding were worth the time and effort?
- ♡ What did I wear for something old, new, borrowed, and blue?
- ♡ Who was in the wedding party, and what was memorable to each of them?
- ♡ What touched our families the most?
- ♡ Who said or did something that was unforgettable?

Enjoying Your Big Day

(At a wedding in Cana, Jesus turned the water into wine.)

> *The master of the banquet tasted the water*
> *that had been turned into wine. . . .*
> *He called the bridegroom aside and said,*
> *"Everyone brings out the choice wine first*
> *and then the cheaper wine . . .*
> *but you have saved the best till now."*
> *—from John 2:9-10*

With all the great food at receptions, it's a shame that most newlyweds are too busy socializing and taking pictures to get a bite of the meal.

Ask your caterer, or a friend, to pack a picnic basket full of the evening's delights. You can enjoy a fabulous feast in your hotel room later that night.

So they are no longer two,
but one.
Therefore what God has joined together,
let man not separate.

—Matthew 19:6

You have just thrown the celebration of a lifetime. You are now officially husband and wife. Use the words *newlywed* and *bride* as long as you can. Bask in the joy of your marriage, and continue celebrating this day forever.

Enjoying Your Big Day

Celebrate this momentous day by honoring those who helped make it all happen.

- ♥ Have flowers delivered the day after the wedding to both sets of parents.
- ♥ Take a picture with each bridesmaid to present later as a thank you gift.
- ♥ Write a quick note to the officiants, thanking them for their part in the day.
- ♥ Include a picture in the thank you note sent to the vendors you used.
- ♥ Make a toast at your reception to the out-of-town guests in attendance.

May they be brought to complete unity
to let the world know that you sent me
and have loved them even as you have loved me.
—John 17:23

Enjoying Your Big Day

Now you will feel no rain,
For each of you will be shelter to the other.
Now you will feel no cold,
For each of you will be warmth to the other.
Now there is no more loneliness,
For each of you will be companion to the other.
Now you are two bodies,
But there is only one life before you.
Go now to your dwelling place
To enter into the days of your togetherness
And may your days be good and long upon the earth.
—Apache Wedding Prayer

Living Happily Ever After

The veil is off, the rice is thrown, the cake is eaten, and the gifts are unwrapped. But this is not the end. Your wedding marks the beginning of a whole new life together—a special season of love.

Becoming One

Congratulations!

With the wedding planning behind you, relax and enjoy your life together. It's time to begin your own chapter of happily ever after. Unlike the fairy tales, some effort is required to make this happen. You can ensure marital bliss by keeping your marriage the top priority in your life.

Merging two individual lives into one isn't always an easy task. Ask the Lord for wisdom in how to adjust. Find trusted friends who have walked this road already to provide you with a listening ear and helpful advice.

Continue to date one another even though you are married. If you view your relationship as comfortable, you will become complacent. Keep striving to surprise, entice, and woo one another. As you walk toward the future together, always remember to hold each other's hand.

A wife is a gift bestowed upon man
to reconcile him to the loss of paradise.

—*Johann Wolfgang von Goethe*

Living Happily Ever After

Your home can be a place for dying or living,
for wilting or blooming,
for anxiety or peace,
for discouragement or affirmation,
for criticism or approval,
for profane disregard or reverence,
for suspicion or trust,
for blame or forgiveness,
for alienation or closeness,
for violation or respect,
for carelessness or caring.
By your daily choices, you will make your home what you want it to be.

—Carole Streeter

It is a fusion of two hearts—
the union of two lives—
the coming together of two tributaries,
which after being joined in marriage,
will flow in the same channel in the same direction . . .
carrying the same burdens of
responsibility and obligation.
—*Peter Marshall*

Living Happily Ever After

Many people say they want a house of peace. How can you accomplish that? The following "dos and don'ts" are a good start:

1. Don't go to bed angry.
2. Don't leave the room when arguing.
3. Don't belittle your spouse.
4. Don't rely on your spouse to meet all your needs.
5. Don't use the phrases "you always" or "you never".
6. Do ask for forgiveness.
7. Do listen attentively.
8. Do respond with loving honesty.
9. Do pray together.
10. Do make time to have fun and laugh.

Marriages may be made in heaven, but people
are responsible for the maintenance work.

—Barbara Johnson

Living Happily Ever After

Give them wisdom and devotion
    in the ordering of their common life,
    that each may be to the other a strength in need,
    a counselor in perplexity,
    a comfort in sorrow,
    and a companion in joy.
Grant that their wills may be so knit together in your will,
    and their spirits in your Spirit,
    that they may grow in love and peace with you and one another
    all the days of their life.

—From *The Book of Common Prayer*

For where two or three come together in my name,
there am I with them.

—*Matthew 18:20*

Unity in a household begins with intertwined hearts. Take the time to join your hearts by praying together, discussing your feelings, and dreaming new goals for your future.

God, the best maker of all marriages,
Combine your hearts in one!
—*Shakespeare*

And over all these virtues put on love,
which binds them all together in perfect unity.
—*Colossians 3:14*

It is no mistake that
maturity *and* matrimony
come from the same Latin word.
—Les and Leslie Parrot

Living Happily Ever After

Doug and Margie held hands as they walked toward the front of the auditorium for the first meeting of the conference. A small kiss was placed on Margie's cheek before Doug rose to the lectern. Her eyes never left him as he delivered his presentation. Once again he shared a story of how much he valued his relationship with his wife. There wasn't a dry eye in the house.

Throughout the week, conference attendees observed the two together. Even if Doug and Margie were across the room from one another, they were still connected. Conversing with either one of them would lead to a statement or two about the positive traits of his or her spouse. Never was a harsh or critical word spoken. Before departing from one another to attend separate meetings, there was a short exchange of sweet words and a soft kiss.

Often mistaken for newlyweds, Doug and Margie proudly share they are still on their honeymoon and have been—for 25+ years.

You are my husband.

My feet shall run because of you.

My feet dance because of you.

My heart shall beat because of you.

My eyes see because of you.

My mind thinks because of you.

And I shall love because of you.

—*Eskimo Love Song*

Embrace the freedom that marriage can bring. Visit places you've always wanted to see. Take a class together at a local college. Pursue dreams you want to come true. Use the strength of each other to experience life to the fullest.

A good marriage relationship is the
foundation of a good sexual relationship.
—*Dr. Barbara Chesser*

Let him kiss me with the kisses of his mouth
—for your love is more delightful than wine.
Pleasing is the fragrance of your perfumes;
your name is like perfume poured out.
No wonder the maidens love you!
Take me away with you—let us hurry!
Let the king bring me into his chambers.

—Song of Songs 1:2-4

Living Happily Ever After

To arouse your spouse and enhance the mood, set the scene for romance:

- ♥ Wear new lingerie.
- ♥ Serve breakfast in bed.
- ♥ Re-create your proposal.
- ♥ Watch a romantic movie.
- ♥ Plan a candlelight dinner.
- ♥ Eat dessert under the stars.
- ♥ Dance in your living room.
- ♥ Watch your wedding video.
- ♥ Prepare a bubble bath for two.

The real mystery of marriage is not
that husband and wife love each other
but that God loves them so much
that they can discover each other more
and more as living reminders of His divine presence.

—Henri Nouwen

Successful marriage is always a triangle:
a man, a woman, and God.

—*Cecil Myers*

Each one of you also must love
his wife as he loves himself,
and the wife must respect her husband.

—*Ephesians 5:33*

I See Jesus In You
by Sharalee Lucas

I used to think how wonderful
to have been here on the earth
When Jesus Christ the Son of God
was born of a human birth.
But nothing could exceed the view
of seeing Jesus born in you
I'll never long for yesterday again.

I see Jesus in your eyes
and it makes me love you.
I feel Jesus in your touch
and I know He cares.
I hear Jesus in your voice

and it makes me listen.
And I'll trust you with my love because you're His.

I see Him,
I see Him in you.

I used to think how wonderful
to meet Him in the air
Then how great the mansions
He's preparing over there.
But now I've come to understand
the Father's perfect master plan
The place He longs to build
is right in you.

A joyful marriage is a bit of heaven on earth.

—Anonymous

Living Happily Ever After

Already the second day since our marriage, his love and gentleness is beyond everything, and to kiss that dear soft cheek, to press my lips to his is heavenly bliss. I feel a purer more unearthly feel than I ever did. Oh! Was ever a woman so blessed as I am?

—Queen Victoria, journal entry from February 12, 1840

Whatever you do,
work at it with all your heart,
as working for the Lord.
—*Colossians 3:23*

Living Happily Ever After

She had a long day at work and couldn't wait to get home. She'd have to figure out something easy for dinner. Leaving her briefcase by the door, she called out to suggest a take-out dinner to her husband.

"In here," he replied from the kitchen. Her senses kicked into overdrive as her nostrils inhaled the aromas of the kitchen.

"What's this?" she asked, pointing to all the pots full of bubbly surprises.

"Dinner for two, my dear."

He brushed his lips across hers and led her to the dining room where she was greeted with a masterpiece. Candles, fine linens, placemats, and a fully set table were before her. He sat her down in front of the setting marked "My love." He rushed to the kitchen and returned with two salad plates filled with luscious greens.

After all five courses were cleared away, he returned with a single red rose. The card simply read, "Just because I love you!"

Celebrate your marriage every minute of every day.

- ♡ During your first year of marriage, celebrate your monthly anniversary by going out to dinner.
- ♡ When you use one of your wedding gifts, share a wedding memory with each other.
- ♡ Schedule a date night each week that is reserved just for the two of you.
- ♡ Pray for each other when you are apart.
- ♡ Leave love notes around the house for each other to find.
- ♡ Watch your wedding video each year on your anniversary.
- ♡ Keep a picture of your spouse in your wallet.

May you have warm words on a cold evening,
a full moon on a dark night,
and the road downhill all the way to your door.
May you be poor in misfortune,
rich in blessings,
slow to make enemies,
quick to make friends.
But rich or poor,
quick or slow,
may you know nothing but happiness
from this day forward.

—Irish Toast

Additional copies of this book
are available at your local bookstore.

If you have enjoyed this book, or if it has
impacted your life, we would like to hear from you.

Please contact us at:
Honor Books
Department E
P.O. Box 55388
Tulsa, Oklahoma 74155

Or by e-mail at info@honorbooks.com